Paloma

Written by **Pat Mora**
Illustrated by **Gerardo Suzán**

Celebration Press
An Imprint of Pearson Learning

"Stop! Stop!" shout Ray and his sisters.
They watch a brown cat run by their house
and down the dirt road.

Ray and his sisters run toward a gray dove.

"Don't scare it," whispers Ray to Lisa and Rita.

"It's hurt," says Rita. "Poor little bird,
pobre pajarito."

They move slowly near the dove.

2

3

"The dove wants to fly, but it can't," says Lisa.

"Poor little dove," says Rita. "We'll take care of you. We'll call you Paloma. That's 'dove' in Spanish."

"Don't scare Paloma," says Ray.

"I'll go get Nina," says Lisa. "Nina can take care of any animal."

4

Lisa runs to find Nina, her grandmother. "Nina, Nina," Lisa calls. "Hurry, we need you! A cat jumped at a dove. Paloma can't fly. We think she's hurt."

Lisa takes Nina's hand. "Ray and Rita are waiting for us," says Lisa.

7

"Pobre pajarito," says Nina. "We'll take care of you."

"Should I bring the cage?" asks Ray.

"Sí, sí, Ray," says Nina. "That's a good idea."

"Should I bring some water and bird seed?" asks Lisa.

"Sí, sí, Lisa," says Nina. "That's a good idea."

Carefully, Nina places Paloma in the cage. "You are safe now, Paloma," she says. "Animals can't hurt you here."

8

9

Every morning Ray, Rita, and Lisa visit Paloma. They bring her fresh water and seed.

"When Paloma can fly," says Nina, "we will have a celebration."

"Yay!" says Ray. "A party, *una fiesta!*"

Every day Rita sits by Paloma's cage and talks to her. "Coo, coo, coo," says Rita.

"Coo, coo, coo," says Paloma.

One day, Rita sees Paloma try to fly in the cage. "Nina! Nina!" she shouts. "Ray! Lisa! Hurry! Paloma wants to fly."

They all run to Paloma's cage. Carefully, Nina lifts the dove out. Paloma walks near the cage, and then . . . she spreads her wings. Paloma flies!

"Look! Paloma is flying!" says Rita.

"It's time for our celebration!" says Nina.

13

The children help Nina set the table outside.

Nina gives each of the children a small, wooden dove she has bought at the market. "Three Palomas," she says.

Then they hear a "Coo, coo, coo."

Look!" says Rita. "It's Paloma!"

14

15

"She's come to her own party," laughs Lisa.